001

00?

00J

UU4

D0G06423

0001_C

005

006

007

008

0002_A

0002_B

0002_C

009

010

011

012

0003_A

0003_B

0003_C

013

014

015

016

0004_A

0004_B

0004_C

017

018

019

020

0005_A

0005_B

0005_C

021

022

023

024

0006_A

0006_B

0006_C

Time & Space Library
please return this book on, or before, the date stamped below

class no. 2065-4379 X721

02 OCT 1992	05 OCT 1994	04 AUG 1999
25 DEC 1992	17 MAR 1995	APR 2000
17 JAN 1993	29 MAR 1995	25 OCT 2000
23 FEB 1993	26 JUN 1995	24 NOV 2000
09 APR 1993	26 NOV 1995	20 DEC 2000
28 JUN 1993	16 FEB 1996	10 JUN 2002
09 AUG 1993	21 MAR 1996	AUG 2002
08 NOV 1993	21 SEP 1996	SEP 2002
21 FEB 1994	31 JAN 1997	SEP 2003
26 APR 1994	08 SEP 1997	SEP 2003
22 JUN 1994	10 DEC 1998	OCT 2003
11 SEP 1994	13 MAR 1999	

How to Create
A Flawless Universe™

IN JUST EIGHT DAYS

godfather publications

godfather publications

Published by godfather publications Ltd

First Published 5976 b.t.
Published in godfather publications Genesis Library 5892 b.t.
Reprinted in godfather publications Classics 5812 b.t.
This edition published 5738 b.t.

11   9   12   12   25 9   19   1   6   15   23

Introduction and Notes copyright © author unknown, 5738 b.t.
Smith Chronology copyright © author unknown, 5812 b.t.

Printed at an undisclosed location

How to Create
A Flawless Universe™

IN JUST EIGHT DAYS

godfather publications

WELCOME!

Congratulations—you've made a jolly good choice by purchasing this manual, and indeed you may soon have many people thanking you for doing so.

In just eight days (also known as a week) you could be ruling your very own flawless Universe™. By following the instructions correctly, you can achieve the type of perfection that other deities only dream of. Day by day and task by task, your universe will unfold before you.

In order to successfully construct a flawless Universe™ you must complete the instructions on ALL eight days. Failure to do so could have catastrophic consequences and leave you stuck with a faulty and wholly unsatisfactory Universe™. Do not fear, however, if things start to go pear shaped—you always have the eighth day to turn to.

Good Luck

The Authors

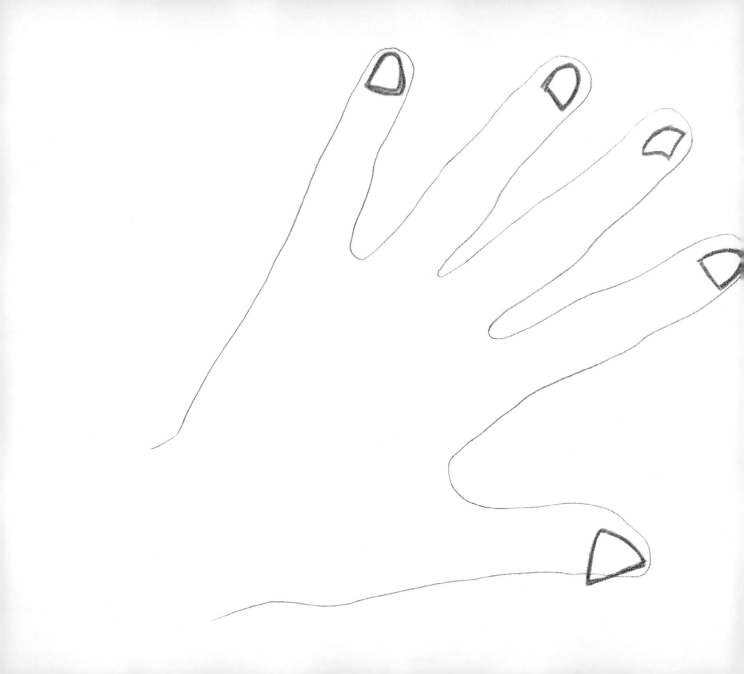

CONTENTS

??

& on the first day

big bang, universe & planets

The Big Bang™ Experiment

This experiment is designed to create what is known as the "Big Bang." The process involves combining a mixture of water and banging powder with a material called "plasticine" and gently heating it until it reaches a very high temperature. This creates a giant explosion, which when poured onto an empty plane results in the creation of a phenomena that we will call a "Universe." *For correspondence between Universes see the eighth day.*

EQUIPMENT
1 Bunsen burner
1 test tube
1 thermometer
1 beaker
1 measuring glass
1 bottle of banging powder
1 lump of plasticine
1 quart of water

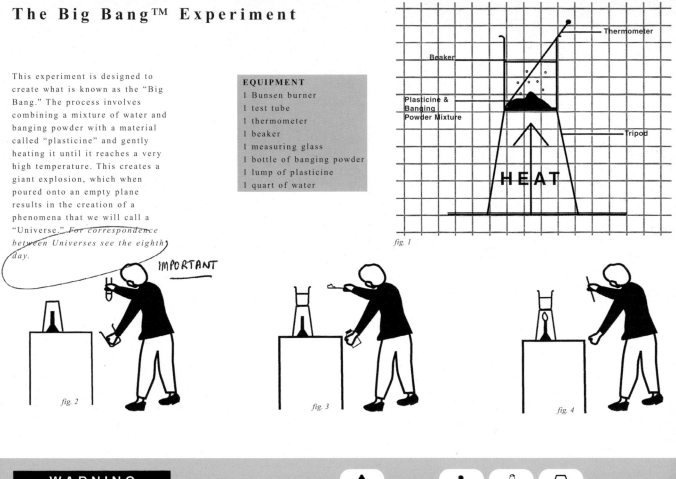

Thermometer
Beaker
Plasticine & Banging Powder Mixture
Tripod
HEAT
fig. 1

IMPORTANT

fig. 2

fig. 3

fig. 4

What to do:

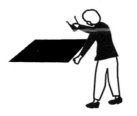

- First mix 1 spatula of banging powder with .5 oz. of water in the test tube until it forms a paste (*fig. 2*).
- Measure 2.75 oz. of water and carefully add the banging powder paste a little at a time (*fig. 3*). Mix well.
- Place the beaker containing the mixture on the tripod and turn the Bunsen burner to a low flame (*fig. 4*).
- Gently heat until it reaches 194°F. Then add 17 oz. of plasticine. Continue heating until it reaches boiling point.
- Carefully remove from the heat.
- For color and texture information refer to chart.

The mixture is now complete. Pour carefully into the empty plane that will be your Universe.

The Development of Your Universe™

At first your Universe will resemble a flat, empty plane. This will be the canvas on which you will create your masterpiece.

Once you have poured the mixture over the plane there will be an almighty BANG! and a flash of light. Make sure you follow all safety instructions to avoid injury.

After the explosion there will be a huge cloud of hot gases and dust. There will be limited visibility and high risk of flying debris. This will take awhile to clear.

CAUTION	CAUTION	CAUTION
LOUD BANG	HOT GASES	FLYING DEBRIS

Creating Your Planets™

Wait until the dust has settled and the hot gases begin to cool. You will be left with hundreds of pieces of matter flying and swirling around (*fig. 1*). This matter is the main component of your planets. To create each planet, take several pieces of matter and mold them together using your hands (See *fig. 2*). Try to make your planets as soon as possible while the matter is still hot as it will be soft and flexible and easier to work with.

The shape you are aiming for is a Sphere. Take care not to make the surface too rough as this can look untidy.

Once you have molded a range of planets place them in the arrangement shown below. In order to differentiate between the planets decorate each one using planet paint (not watercolors as they fade quickly) as shown in *fig. 3*. Examples of colors and patterns are shown on the color chart. You may wish to add further decorations such as rings and fuzzy glows.

Use the boxes on the opposite page to design and name your planets.

Choose a planet to call Earth. This will be the one you will be focusing on for the rest of the creation process.

For details on duplicating creation on other planets see the eighth day.

fig. 1

like your jumper – new?

MVROERE

fig. 2   fig. 3

Mine looks like this!

Naming Your Planets™

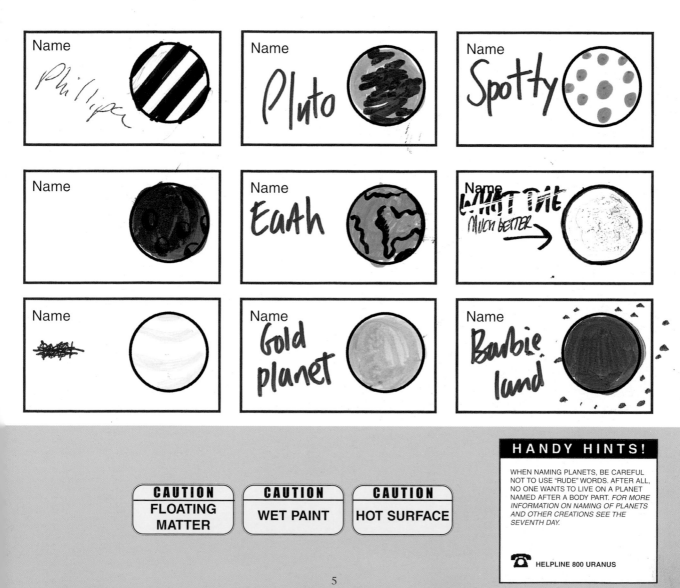

Name **Phillipa**

Name **Pluto**

Name **Spotty**

Name

Name **Eath**

Name ~~WHAT THE~~ *MUCH BETTER* →

Name ~~(scribble)~~

Name **Gold planet**

Name **Barbie land**

HANDY HINTS!

WHEN NAMING PLANETS, BE CAREFUL NOT TO USE "RUDE" WORDS. AFTER ALL, NO ONE WANTS TO LIVE ON A PLANET NAMED AFTER A BODY PART. *FOR MORE INFORMATION ON NAMING OF PLANETS AND OTHER CREATIONS SEE THE SEVENTH DAY.*

☎ HELPLINE 800 URANUS

The Cosmic Glow™

As you complete the painting and naming process, begin to hang each planet to dry overnight *(fig. 1)*. As you hang them, set them to spin a little to encourage an even finish.

For instructions on eternal planet spinning see the eighth day.

To create a cosmic glow place temporary lighting above them. This will encourage the processes known as "day" and "night."

A more permanent source of light will be created on the fourth day.

Once the planets are totally dry, take the planet chosen as your Earth and dissect through the center. Spoon out the inside and fill with water. Then reseal with a strong glue. Make sure you do this properly as cracks may cause problems in the future.

WHAT ON EARTH HAPPENED HERE?

Please = Beware dripping paint.

CAUTION
BRIGHT LIGHT

There was NO BANG!
I didn't just like the
instructions said —I think.

idiot — MY BANG was HUGE

PLanets won't dry.

There are big puddles everywhere.

AREFH? REATH HEART
ATHER? EAKTH TRAET

SOURCE OF LIGHT

Banging Powder —$3.99
(x25)

LIGHT NIGHTS?
DARK DAYS?

BANG

everything should sparkle,

NIGHT

EVENING

DAY

 **on the second day**

separating the waters

Separating the Waters™

At this stage the Earth that you created on *the first day* should be entirely covered with water. Now you have to separate the water, so there is some on the Earth's surface and some surrounding the Earth.

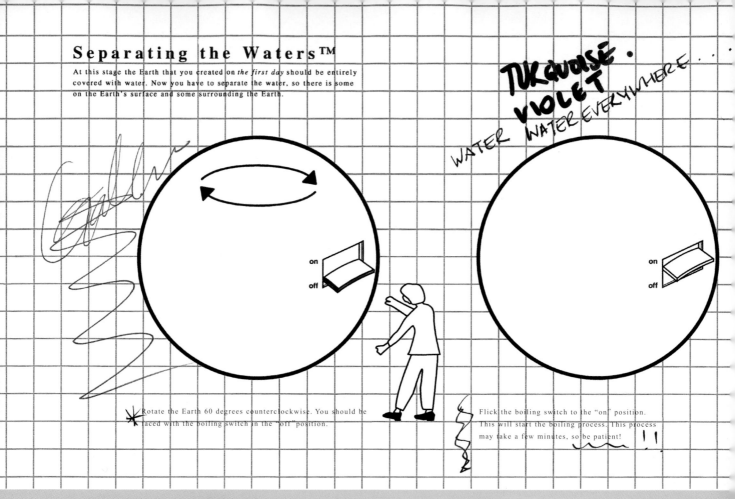

Rotate the Earth 60 degrees counterclockwise. You should be faced with the boiling switch in the "off" position.

Flick the boiling switch to the "on" position. This will start the boiling process. This process may take a few minutes, so be patient!

10

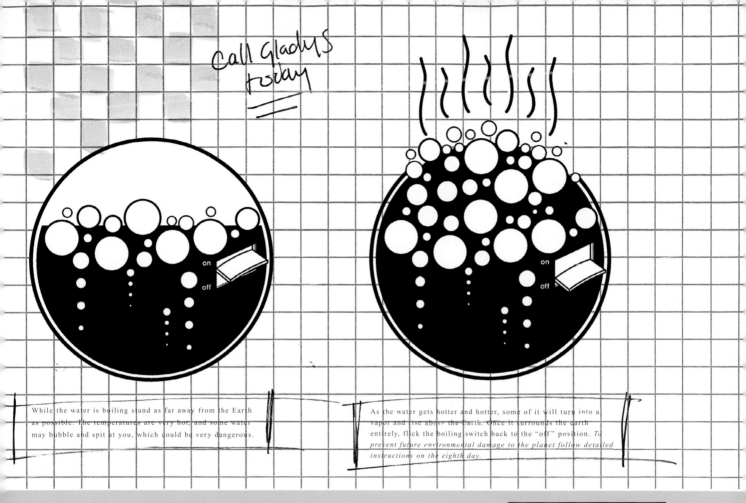

While the water is boiling stand as far away from the Earth as possible. The temperatures are very hot, and some water may bubble and spit at you, which could be very dangerous.

As the water gets hotter and hotter, some of it will turn into a vapor and rise above the Earth. Once it surrounds the earth entirely, flick the boiling switch back to the "off" position. *To prevent future environmental damage to the planet follow detailed instructions on the eighth day.*

CAUTION
STEAM

CAUTION
HOT SURFACE

HANDY HINTS!

TAKE CARE TO WEAR PROTECTIVE GLOVES WHEN HANDLING THE EARTH AS IT WILL BE EXTREMELY HOT. AVOID RISING VAPOR BY WEARING A PROTECTIVE MASK AT ALL TIMES.

☎ HELPLINE 800 SNUGGLY

Coloring the Sky™

At this stage, you should have water covering the Earth's surface and water held above the Earth in what we call "clouds." The space in between these two waters is called "sky," and it is yours to color and decorate as you like. Enjoy.
Refer to color chart for paint options.

4.999
6.013
781 3

18.525

001 PAINT SHOPPI

PAINT OPTIONS

matte. → TOO EX 28
→ Chris. TOO SLOW DRYING
John. → US ELE
← gloss. NOT BAD
vinyl. → SCRATC EASIL

Filling the Vacuum™

Now you have chosen your color for the sky you need to fill the space with what we call "waves" and "clouds." Waves belong in the sea and clouds in the sky. Color them as you like. Refer to color chart for ideas and use this page to experiment with possible color combinations.

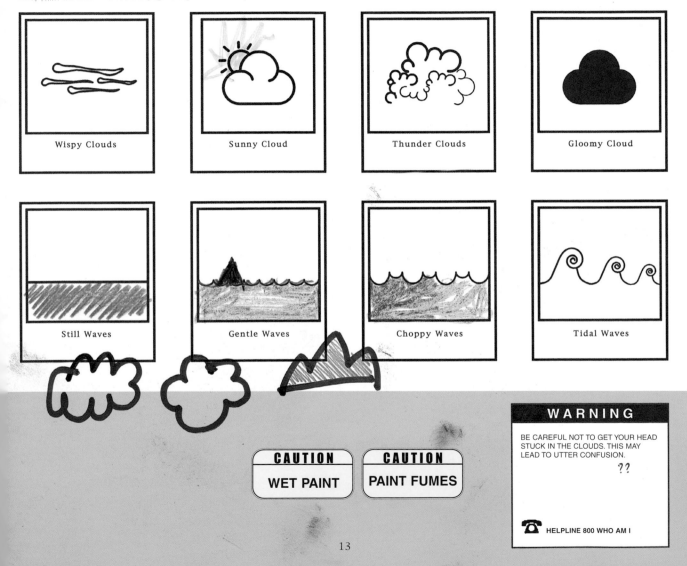

Wispy Clouds

Sunny Cloud

Thunder Clouds

Gloomy Cloud

Still Waves

Gentle Waves

Choppy Waves

Tidal Waves

CAUTION
WET PAINT

CAUTION
PAINT FUMES

WARNING

BE CAREFUL NOT TO GET YOUR HEAD STUCK IN THE CLOUDS. THIS MAY LEAD TO UTTER CONFUSION.

??

☎ HELPLINE 800 WHO AM I

13

Creating Weather™

Now you have sky, clouds, and waves, you need "weather" to give you something to do with them. *For more information about when to implement all weather systems see the eighth day.*

LIGHTNING *LETHAL STUFF!*

To create lightning take one hair dryer, plug it into an electricity supply, and drop the hair dryer into a bath or some other receptacle containing water. Sparks will fly.

RAIN

To create rain first situate yourself in an enclosed area—this is vital for maximum effect. Then take ten large onions and chop or dice into small pieces. The fumes from the onions will make your eyes stream with water. Simply aim this water over Earth and you will have the rain.

RAINBOW

To create a rainbow load a bow and arrow with seven arrows. On the end of each arrow you need miniature paint pots with seven different colors of paint. Fire the arrows in an arch shape and watch the colors form a beautiful rainbow over the Earth.

SNOW

To create snow take five bean bags and remove the innards from the cover. Then take a large knife and carefully slash a long split into each bag and empty the contents over the Earth. This should cover earth with a beautiful white powder.

CLOUD

To create clouds take one smoking pipe and light it with great care. A puff of smoke will rise from the end of it—this can also be referred to as a "cloud" of smoke. Gently blow the clouds around the Earth to occasionally block out the sun.

WIND

For full-force wind, first consume eight tins of baked beans. For a more gentle breeze, reduce the number of tins consumed accordingly. Allow one hour for the beans to be digested and then let rip. Warning: You may need to hold your nose.

HAIL

To create hail, ensure that Earth's temperatures are very cold, preferably below 32°F. Fill a firing machine with frozen rain (see column two for how to create rain); once the rain has frozen it is then called "hail." Aim firing machine toward the Earth, being careful to spread the hail evenly.

SLEET

To create sleet you need a large mixing bowl and a wooden spoon. Mix together two parts rain and one part snow until a mush has formed in the bowl. Push the mush through a sieve over the earth. This is what we call "sleet."

8x tins beans

CAUTION
ELECTRICITY

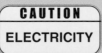

CALLING ALL GOATS... CALLING ALL GOATS!!

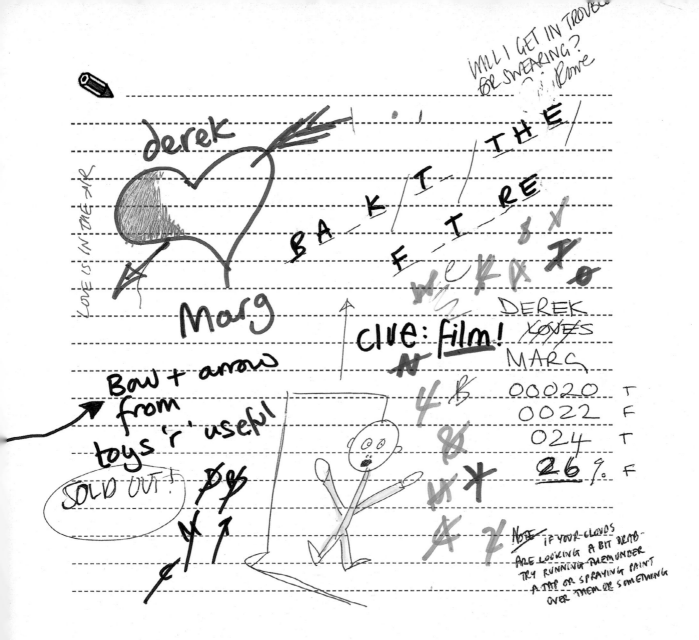

& on the third day

land & vegetation

Creating the Landmass™

For Global Separation, a great deal of care must be taken. As highlighted by the red circles, keep your eye on the globe.

fig. 1

At this point the globe is a fully operational ball of saltwater *(See the second day for creation of ball of saltwater)*. It is essential that the globe is delicately separated. The best line of separation is one known as the "equator," a line found by cutting through the center of the globe.

   To separate, firmly hold the top and bottom and twist the top section clockwise. Assure there is no spillage, as this may cause shallow oceans.

fig. 2

Once it is separated, rest the globe on a flat surface and begin to drain the saltwater from the inside. For this, we advise a large ladle (available from most leading galaxies). The extracted saltwater may be used to create lakes and puddles. Leave between one and six miles of saltwater around the circumference of the globe. This leaves plenty of room for plant life and creatures that feel inclined to get in the oceans and have a bit of a paddle. *(See the fifth day for marine activities.)*

fig. 3

The final stage is critical for human survival. The stages of construction are below:
(Approx. weights in brackets are in kilograms.)

1. the crust (5.974×10^7)
2. the solid convecting mantle (5.974×10^{12})
3. liquid outer core (5.974×10^{10})
4. the solid inner core (5.974×10^5)

my liquid outer core hardened mid-way through the 6th day and trapped all the sea creatures

Keep your eye on the globe at all times, as a dropped globe can cause . . . *(see the eighth day for aid in recovery of a dropped globe.)*

1

PURPLE RINSE Luvie

2

3

It is critical that each stage is allowed to set for at least ten minutes. This will allow the crust to develop. Full development will take one day—this is required to create between five and seven landmasses.

(INDEED)

Sensible footwear is a must when dealing with landfill.

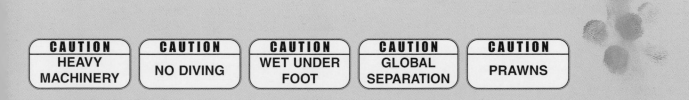

CAUTION	CAUTION	CAUTION	CAUTION	CAUTION
HEAVY MACHINERY	NO DIVING	WET UNDER FOOT	GLOBAL SEPARATION	PRAWNS

Creating Vegetation™

fig. 1
Looking at the fruit created, the body (otherwise known as the flesh) can often be soft and moist. The moisture created by water must be kept on the inside of the fruit. See *fig. 2* for the creation of skin.

fig. 2
Looking at the fruit created, the skin (otherwise known as the outside) can often be hard and crispy. The crunch created by small crunch particles must be kept on the inside of the fruit. See *fig. 3* for creation of stalk.

fig. 3
The stalk is the simple means of attaching the vegetation to the piece of plant life from which it was born. This plant life comes in many forms—under the land, on the land, and over the land. *Refer to color chart for examples of textures and colors.* This task can at times be ever so tortuous. Be very careful not to slip up.

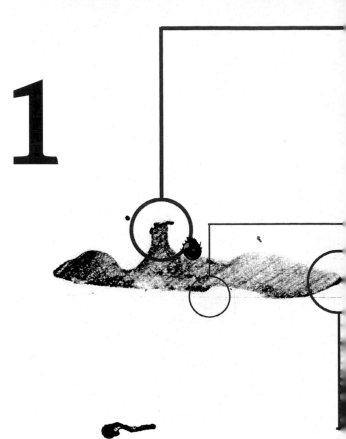

→ MAIL FROM THE 'GRAPE ACTION' HELPLINE WAS EXTREMELY RODE, <u>AND</u> I COULDN'T UNDERSTAND HIM.

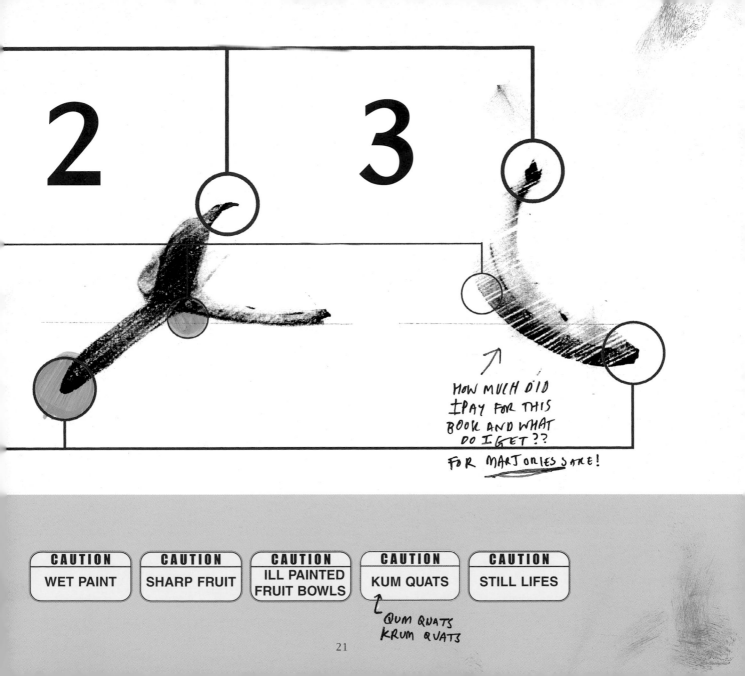

2 3

HOW MUCH DID
I PAY FOR THIS
BOOK AND WHAT
DO I GET ??

FOR MARJORIES SAKE!

CAUTION	CAUTION	CAUTION	CAUTION	CAUTION
WET PAINT	SHARP FRUIT	ILL PAINTED FRUIT BOWLS	KUM QUATS	STILL LIFES

QUM QUATS
KRUM QUATS

Looking Deeper at Vegetation™

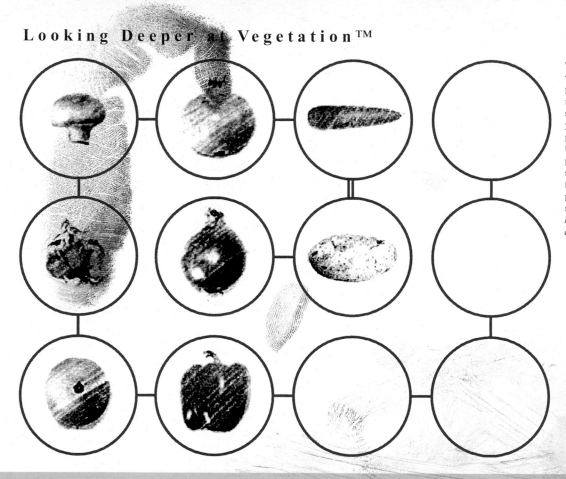

When creating the wide variety of vegetation, please choose large ranges of sizes and shapes. This will keep your customer (the persons) wide-eyed. Using the color chart provided, "go wild" when selecting the colors. It is imperative that any production of sprouts is reported. *If sprouts are located, see the eighth day for their destruction.*

HANDY HINTS!

WE HAVE HEARD RUMORS THAT THE PRODUCTION OF SPROUTS HAVE INFILTRATED THE MAINSTREAM OF VEGETATION PRODUCTION IN SOME UNIVERSE ATTEMPTS. IF ANY SPROUTS ARE SEEN, PLEASE REPORT THEM TO THE CONTACT NUMBER BELOW.

 HELPLINE 800 SPROUTS

NOTE TO READER

In an attempt to create the banana™, i found that my people just kept on slipping on the banana "skins"... **BIG PROBLEM** just thought i'd let you all know

* banana skins can kill !!!!

I FIND THAT A TRUMP A DAY KEEPS LOVED ONES AWAY
MR L.

* why do i need a lampshade?

IMPORTANT
YOU SHOULD ALWAYS KEEP ONE STEP AHEAD.

GOT THIS FROM THE EIGHTH DAY- UNBELIEVABLE !

HE IS

& on the fourth day

galaxies, stars & time

The Universe™

Your Universe—a flat plane—will slide into the cosmos at your requested coordinates. You must simply choose your types of "galaxies," "systems," and "planets."

Timeline—used for passage via wormholes between different Universes

Universe (x1)

I'M CONFUSED.

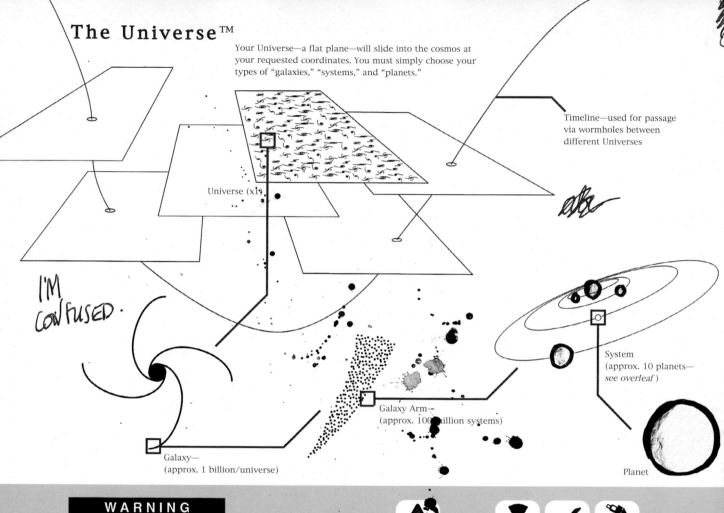

System
(approx. 10 planets—
see overleaf)

Galaxy Arm—
(approx. 100 million systems)

Galaxy—
(approx. 1 billion/universe)

Planet

Galaxies™

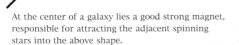

At the center of a galaxy lies a good strong magnet, responsible for attracting the adjacent spinning stars into the above shape.

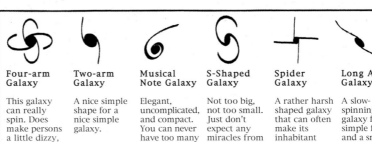

Four-arm Galaxy

This galaxy can really spin. Does make persons a little dizzy, though.

Two-arm Galaxy

A nice simple shape for a nice simple galaxy.

Musical Note Galaxy

Elegant, uncomplicated, and compact. You can never have too many single-arm galaxies.

S-Shaped Galaxy

Not too big, not too small. Just don't expect any miracles from this most "average" of galaxies.

Spider Galaxy

A rather harsh shaped galaxy that can often make its inhabitant persons a little bit unpleasant.

Long Arm Galaxy

A slow-spinning galaxy for simple folk and a small community spirit.

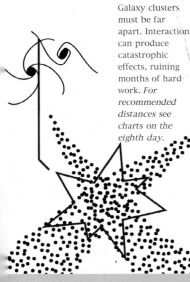

Galaxy clusters must be far apart. Interaction can produce catastrophic effects, ruining months of hard work. *For recommended distances see charts on the eighth day.*

Galaxy™ Creation

fig. 1 Take a strong magnet and suspend in space.

fig. 2 Sprinkle lightly with stars.

fig. 3 Sit back and watch as stars begin to take shape around the magnet. *Refer to color chart.*

fig. 4

You should then apply a second magnet to attract one arm of your static galaxy. As it begins to spin, it will take shape.

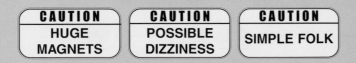

Star Systems™

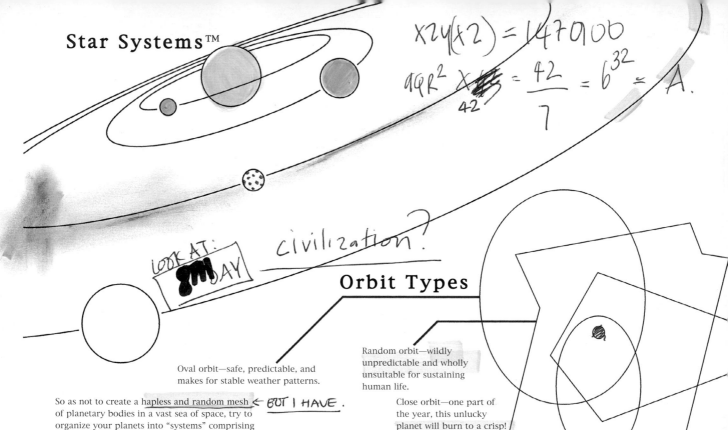

$$X24(x2) = 147000$$
$$99R^2 \times \cancel{42} = \frac{42}{7} = 6^{32} = A.$$

LOOK AT: ~~8TH~~ DAY ← civilization?

Orbit Types

Oval orbit—safe, predictable, and makes for stable weather patterns.

Random orbit—wildly unpredictable and wholly unsuitable for sustaining human life.

So as not to create a hapless and random mesh ← BUT I HAVE. of planetary bodies in a vast sea of space, try to organize your planets into "systems" comprising five to ten bodies. Choose from different planet types for an interesting range. *For notes on proximity of inhabited planets and difficulty of contact between civilizations see the eighth day.*

Close orbit—one part of the year, this unlucky planet will burn to a crisp!

Star Types and Core Makeup

Circular Star

The circular star really isn't that interesting. Persons tend to be decidely unimpressed with its shape.

Cube Star

The cube star's pointy edges can cause fatal accidents. It can also be intimidating.

Egg Star

Gives persons a sense of comfort. Watch them try and build a religious sun-worshipping temple out of this one!

Pyramid Star

The pyramid star's most irregular shape can cause bizarre weather effects in summer.

Grinning Star

Can go either way. Persons either become impeccably cheerful or horribly ironic.

Confusing to say the least. Tends to "wobble" uncontrollably in the sky

NO

Main Core— composed of molten lava, feeding the furnace of the outer flame.

Outer Flame Layer— to start fire burning, apply flammable chemicals and set alight.

Absolute Center— home of the secret mechanism that keeps systems functioning perfectly. *For notes on its construction see the eighth day*

Protective Layer— layer of hard rock to protect center.

Gaseous planet

Giant planet

Inhabited planet

Star

Asteroid belt

Ringed planet

my asteroids just kept on bumpin' into each other—logistical nightmre

CAUTION	CAUTION	CAUTION
IRONY	ASTRO-PHYSICS	CHEESE MOONS

Time™

Make sure you keep dates simple. Persons don't like to be bothered with obtuse number of months in a year, days in a week, etc.

"Eyes open" time passes normally

"Eyes closed" time stops

2 weeks in 1 month

4 months in 1 year

1 month in 1 year; no weeks

8 weeks in 1 month

2 months in 1 year

1 month in 1 year

The average person should live for between 0 and 100 years. So as not to waste the time they spend living, time should stop when a person becomes unconscious. *For details on correct implementation see the eighth day.* Lifespans can be split up into "Youth" (frivolous), "Middle Age" (productive), and "Old" (reflective). Getting the balance right takes practice but ensures that these three ages complement each other satisfactorily.

Young

Middle Aged

Old

0 years old

100 years old

IF IT WAS DOWN TO ME, I'D FORGET MONDAYS AND JUST HAVE SEVEN [PA...]

CAUTION
MONDAYS

30

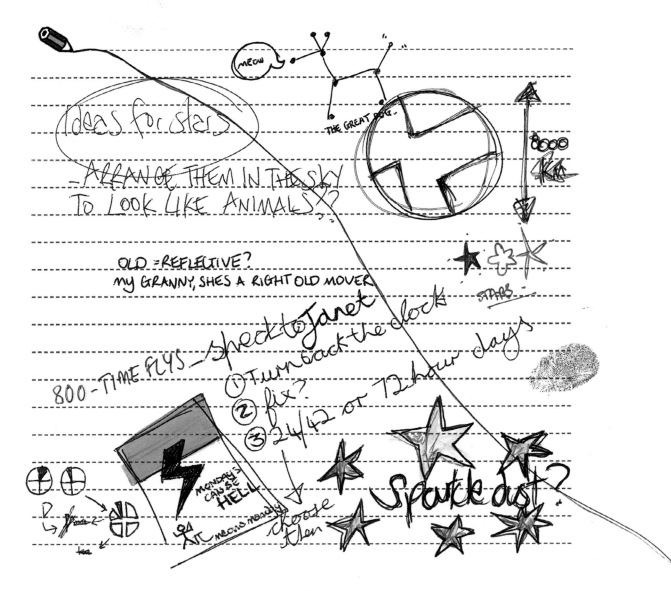

Ideas for stars

- ARRANGE THEM IN THE SKY
TO LOOK LIKE ANIMALS?

MEOW

THE GREAT DOG

8000

STARS

OLD = REFLECTIVE?
MY GRANNY, SHES A RIGHT OLD MOVER

800-TIME FLYS - Sheck to Janet

① Turn back the clock
② fix?
③ 24/42 or 72 hour days

MONDAYS
CAN BE
HELL

MEOW monday

choose
then

Sparkle dust?

&on the fifth day

sea & sky animals

Birds and Sea Creatures™

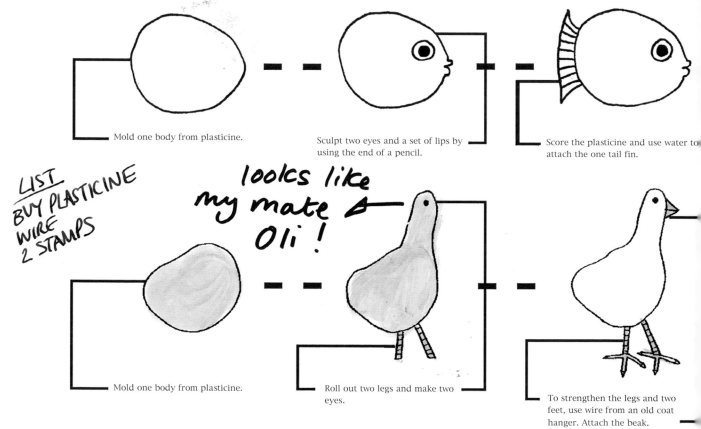

Mold one body from plasticine.

Sculpt two eyes and a set of lips by using the end of a pencil.

Score the plasticine and use water to attach the one tail fin.

LIST
BUY PLASTICINE
WIRE
2 STAMPS

looks like my mate Oli !

Mold one body from plasticine.

Roll out two legs and make two eyes.

To strengthen the legs and two feet, use wire from an old coat hanger. Attach the beak.

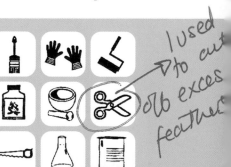

I used to cut ob exces feather

Two fins are simply cut out and stuck on the side of the fish.

Teach the fish to swim.

Cover the body with scales. Use water-resistant paint, selecting your colors from the chart provided. *For full instructions on how to extend their memory span and intellect see the eighth day.*

A tail will give the bird balance and be useful for flying.

Add two wings. Teach bird to fly.

Smother with adhesive and dip in feathers. Use water-resistant paint. *For tips on preventing extinction see the eighth day.*

IT BIT ME!!-OW!

CAUTION	CAUTION	CAUTION
WET PAINT	GOGGLES REQUIRED	AVOID SKIN CONTACT

WARNING

MAKE SURE BOTH SPECIES ARE SATURATED IN PAINT TO ENSURE SURVIVAL IN WATER. YOU WOULDN'T WANT THE WHOLE THING TO GO SHODDILY AFTER ALL YOUR HARD WORK, WOULD YOU?

☎ HELPLINE 800 RAIN PROOF

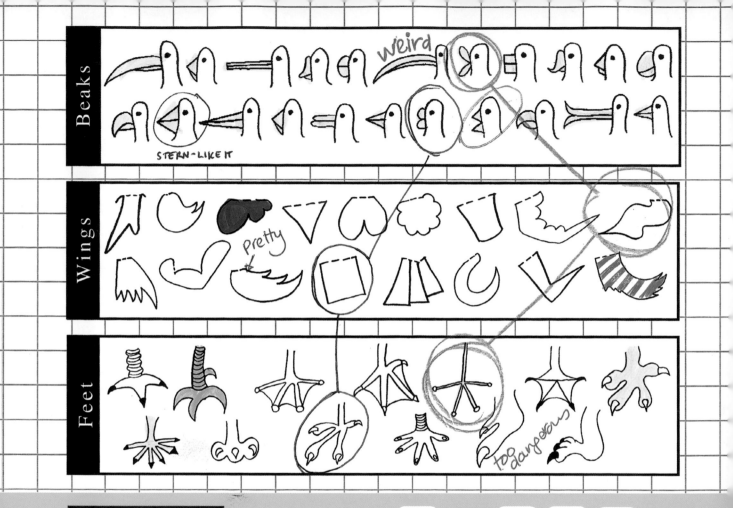

Beaks

weird

STERN-LIKE IT

Wings

Pretty

Feet

too dangerous

Creating Different Species™

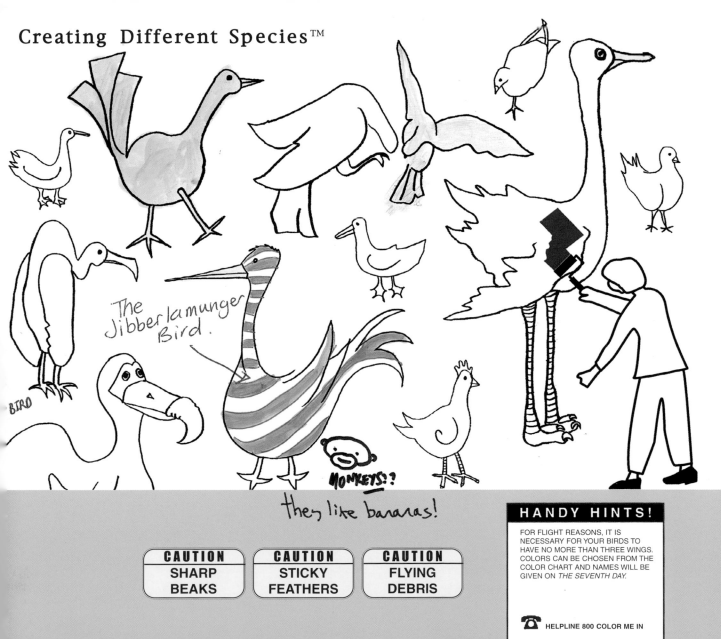

The Jibberlamunger Bird.

BIRD

MONKEYS??

they like bananas!

CAUTION	CAUTION	CAUTION
SHARP BEAKS	STICKY FEATHERS	FLYING DEBRIS

HANDY HINTS!

FOR FLIGHT REASONS, IT IS NECESSARY FOR YOUR BIRDS TO HAVE NO MORE THAN THREE WINGS. COLORS CAN BE CHOSEN FROM THE COLOR CHART AND NAMES WILL BE GIVEN ON *THE SEVENTH DAY*.

☎ HELPLINE 800 COLOR ME IN

Shell

Scales

Other

good shape

NOT PRACTICAL

could use for something else?

HANDY HINTS!

GO ON, GO WILD. DEEP DOWN IN YOUR OCEANS IT'S GOING TO BE DARK, SO YOUR SPECIES OF FISH WON'T BE ABLE TO SEE EACH OTHER ANYWAY, SO IF IT DOES GO SLIGHTLY WRONG, JUST COUNT IT AS A HAPPY MISTAKE.

☎ HELPLINE 800 FISHMONGER

Creating Different Species™

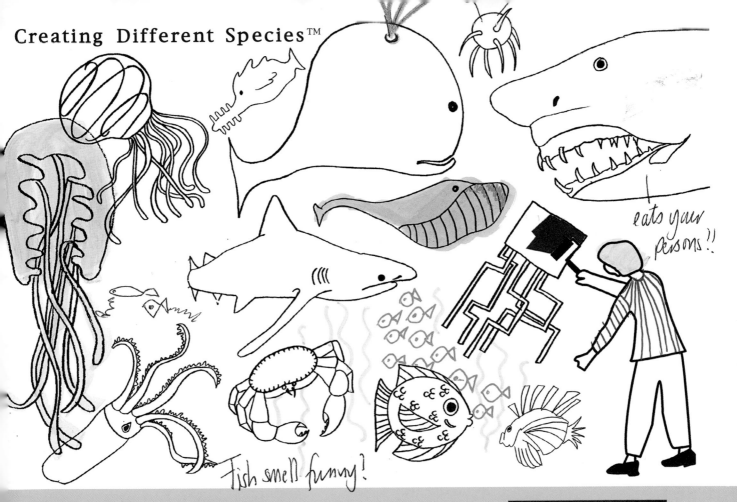

eats your
persons?!

fish smell funny?

CAUTION
SHARP TEETH

CAUTION
ELECTRIC
SHOCKS

CAUTION
DELICATE
SKINS

HANDY HINTS!

COLORS CAN BE CHOSEN FROM THE COLOR CHART AND NAMES WILL BE GIVEN ON *THE SEVENTH DAY*. REMEBER TO HAVE FUN WITH YOUR COLORS. JUST CLOSE YOUR EYES, DIP YOUR BRUSH IN THE BUCKET, AND AWAY YOU GO.

☎ HELPLINE 800 PAINT ME UP

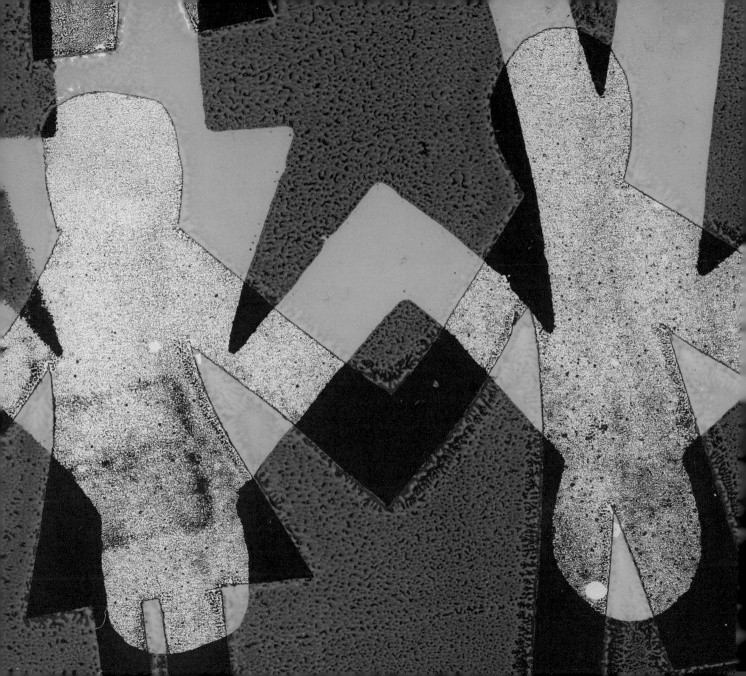

& on the sixth day

persons & animals

Creating Your First Person™

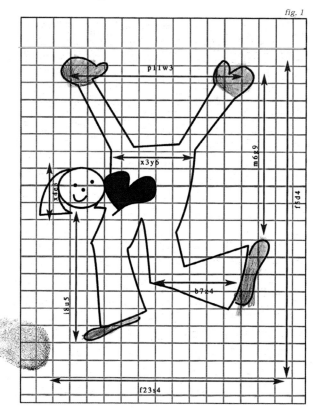

fig. 1

p1lw3

x3y6

m6f9

f5d4

i8u5

b7z4

f23s4

Variables:

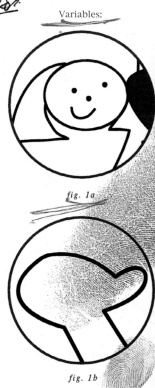

fig. 1a

fig. 1b

Initially two genders of person must be created. It is left up to you to decide if you would like any further additions following their creation.

fig. 1 shows the final result of a male creation. This is for illustrative purposes only—specifications are subject to change depending on creation conditions.

Exterior dimensions are relative to universal dimensions. Ensure all calculations are correct and adhered to—all data is subject to manufacturer's tolerances. *Refer to color chart for color options.*

fig. 1 shows a model with standard equipment plus optional extras detailed on page 46. *For personality control and the "nice factor" see the eighth day.*

How to Make Persons™

fig. 2

fig. 3

fig. 4

melting pot

fig. 5

fig. 6

complete personetta mix

version xxv

fig. 2
Buy your complete person mix from a reputable dealer. Beware of imitations—they can lead to fatal errors in person judgment, which may have harmful results on your universe. *To correct this error see the eighth day.*
fig. 3
Add water to complete person mix, stirring thoroughly and continuously for a little while.
fig. 4
Place beaker over a heater until contents boil over.
fig. 5
Pour liquid into a ready-set container quickly and evenly. Beware of any spills. Leave to settle for a bit longer than you think necessary.
fig. 6
Chip off mold and hang to dry in the garden. Repeat entire process with your second gender choice. *Refer to color chart provided.*

Do not leave a chip on the shoulder of any persons ever, ever.

CAUTION	CAUTION	CAUTION
ANGER	WOMEN	FISTICUFFS

linked

Decisions About Your Animal™ Kingdom

Example: "The Camel" but instructions apply to all models, kangaroos excepted.

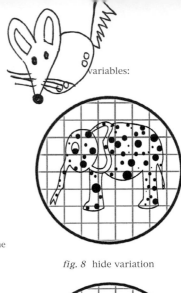

fig. 7

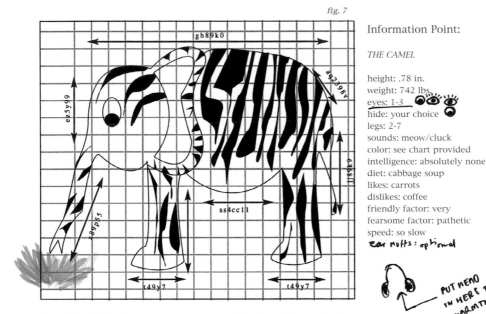

Information Point:

THE CAMEL

height: .78 in.
weight: 742 lbs.
eyes: 1-3
hide: your choice
legs: 2-7
sounds: meow/cluck
color: see chart provided
intelligence: absolutely none
diet: cabbage soup
likes: carrots
dislikes: coffee
friendly factor: very
fearsome factor: pathetic
speed: so slow
ear mufs: optional

PUT MEMO IN HERE FOR WARMTH

variables:

fig. 8 hide variation

fig. 9 the monkey

mine looks NOTHING like this — its so much better

Your Animal Kingdom must be compatible with persons. There should be a healthy animosity between certain varieties. Mix and match all species with relevant surroundings. Ensure there is enough food to feed everybody - animals have a tendency to kill when hungry, not a pleasant sight for you or your persons. *For a good hierarchy structure, refer to the eighth day.*

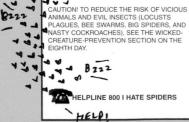

WARNING

CAUTION! TO REDUCE THE RISK OF VICIOUS ANIMALS AND EVIL INSECTS (LOCUSTS PLAGUES, BEE SWARMS, BIG SPIDERS, AND NASTY COCKROACHES), SEE THE WICKED-CREATURE-PREVENTION SECTION ON THE EIGHTH DAY.

Bzzz

☎ HELPLINE 800 I HATE SPIDERS

HELP!

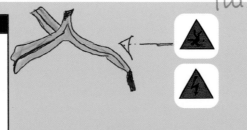

Making Your Animal™ Kingdom

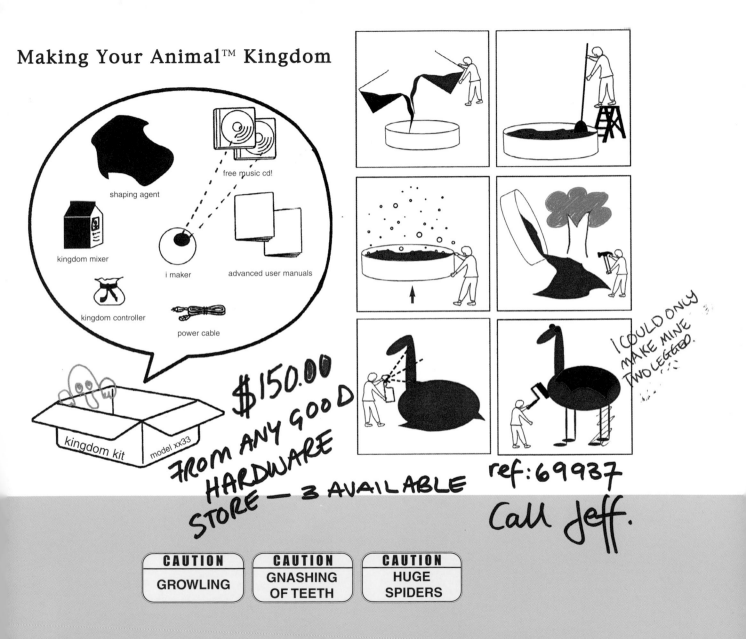

Specification Information

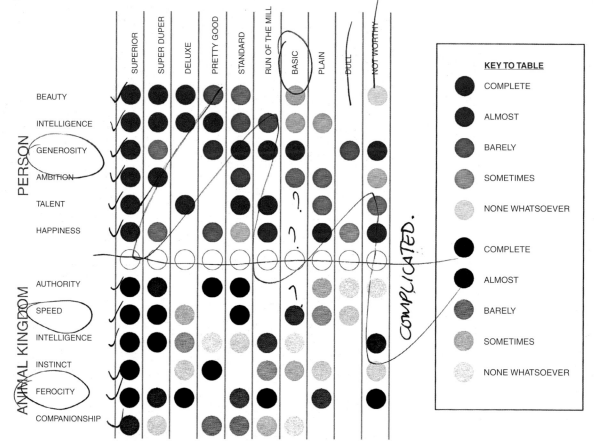

KEY TO TABLE

- COMPLETE
- ALMOST
- BARELY
- SOMETIMES
- NONE WHATSOEVER
- COMPLETE
- ALMOST
- BARELY
- SOMETIMES
- NONE WHATSOEVER

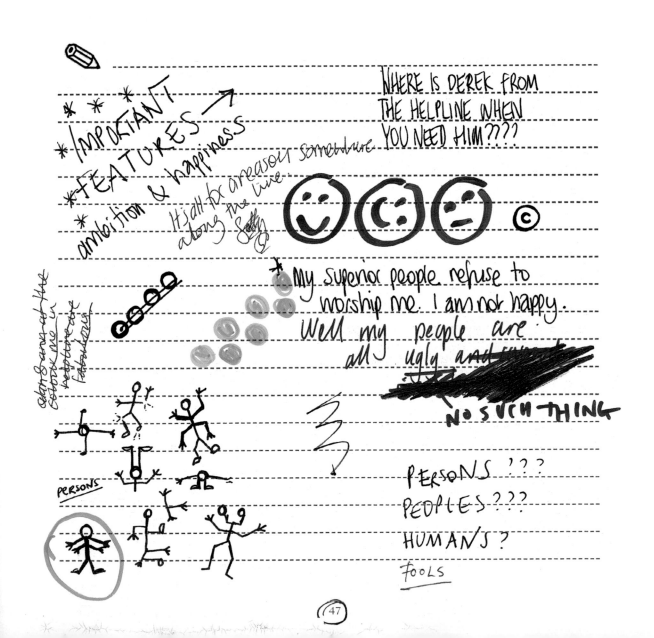

* * *
* IMPORTANT →
* FEATURES →
* ambition & happiness

It's all for a reason somewhere along the line. Sally

WHERE IS DEREK FROM THE HELPLINE WHEN YOU NEED HIM????

©

©

*My superior people refuse to worship me. I am not happy.
Well my people are all ugly and ~~current~~

NO SUCH THING

PERSONS
datey & some at the school. Me in helpline care Fabulosoura

PERSONS '??
PEOPLES ???
HUMANS ?
FOOLS

47

& on the seventh day

relaxing & naming

is anybody else
scared by this image?

How to Name Your Creations™

Of course, you may wish to use the names we have supplied you with to label your many creations.
However, if you do not, simply take an object, choose its category, and make a word from these helpful segments.

Animal™

wat	arto	sula
lod	arde	phila
abr	octo	ngle
erm	inglo	ment
rot	iflo	satet
top	isi	pect
umb	ina	cribe
out	urte	tive
pin	ore	fore

watinglopect

outinangle

Vegetable™

pin	ore	fore
ast	uple	sion
sed	aflo	tent
dim	ebi	site
fam	urgo	stic
gor	opa	later
hal	iflu	vel
lyp	esto	fula
nep	irte	ster

per - - - - - pl - - - ex

perplex

dimoretent

astopafula

Mineral™

spl	ace	thon
cry	urde	plath
mon	ola	sis
scr	oste	sers
ber	elfi	tion
mel	ela	nion
tom	ucto	pint
cat	edo	pass
wat	arto	sula

beracepass

meledoplath

Some Useful Stock Names™

If you are struggling for good names, try using some of these popular examples.

badger	handkerchief	mellifluous	moist
squat *foliage*	mullet	sausage	crayon
plinth	shoes	velcro	artichoke
eyeball		*cloisters*	

avuncular

oceous?

ukulele

sparkle

bean

fuzzy

spatula

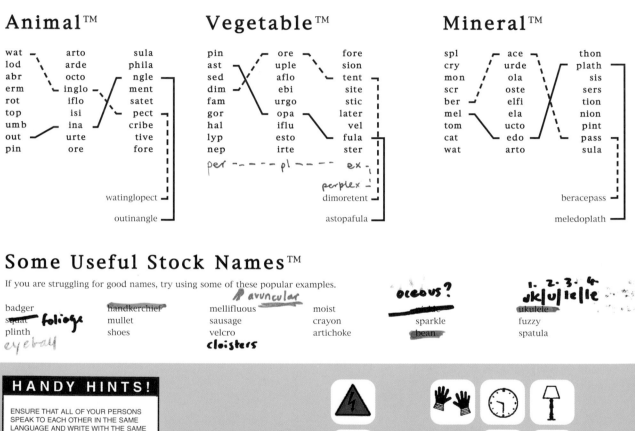

Communication Between Persons™

For persons to communicate with each other, they will need a method of representation of the words they can speak. To do this, pick them a group of symbols from the following list and make them an Alphabet™ to create written words with. Use of 20 to 40 symbols is recommended.

j z = [x 0 © Ω c k \ £ ≈ ; , . 4 < ®

v ? : ø _ + ¡ ™ * # ^ ¢ μ m ● ∞ 6 %

e = a ª 7 – ≠ ' π i ≥ w ^ ¨ 9 ¥ @ }

† ! t s ´ ∑ œ] å 5 ᵖ u n q 8 > ∂ f

(d \ " · Δ r $ æ & 2 q / … h ÷ y

ß ● ∫ 1 ° ç | ≤ § f 3 " ~ √ g +

CHEEKY MONKEY!

CAUTION	CAUTION	CAUTION
SLANG	SILENT G'S	DOUBLE ENTENDRE

WARNING

DON'T MAKE VOCABULARY TOO… INCOMPREHENSIBLE— IT'LL DUMBFOUND YOUR INEXPERIENCED INHABITANTS TO DISTRACTION.

☎ HELPLINE "SEE SPOT RUN"

51

You Have Some Fun™

How to enjoy your new Universe

Don't let it all get to your head—you still have work to do on the pivotal _eighth day._

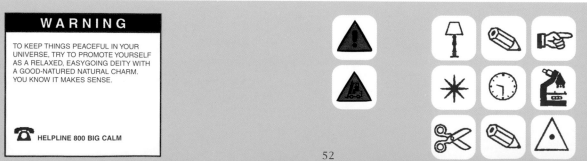

WARNING

TO KEEP THINGS PEACEFUL IN YOUR UNIVERSE, TRY TO PROMOTE YOURSELF AS A RELAXED, EASYGOING DEITY WITH A GOOD-NATURED NATURAL CHARM. YOU KNOW IT MAKES SENSE.

☎ HELPLINE 800 BIG CALM

Put your
feet up,
love.....

CAUTION	CAUTION	CAUTION
OVEREATING	MAD DOGS	ALCOHOLIC BEVERAGES

WARNING

CAUTION! IF YOU DO NOT REMEMBER TO
REGISTER YOUR UNIVERSE, IT WILL BE
DESTROYED BY THE BOARD OF SPACE
AND TIME. NO EXCEPTIONS CAN BE
MADE TO THIS RULE. DO NOT BE
ALARMED—YOUR UNIVERSE WILL BE
"DEALT WITH" LONG BEFORE LIFE HAS
BLOSSOMED. NO HUMANS WILL BE HURT
IN THE ENFORCEMENT OF THIS LAW.

 HELPLINE 800 TOP DOG

Rest, young Marjorie, rest, but don't become too complacent, as there is still work to be done . . .

&on the eighth day

problem ~~solving~~ & ~~coping with~~ chaos
SHARING

Correcting Chaos™

With such a challenging task as creating a Universe™ from scratch, errors may inadvertantly occur. In this chapter we shall endeavor to do all we can to solve any issues or problems you might have encountered.

Past creators have generally found our instructions perfect, so if you didn't manage to complete your Universe™ successfully, please don't even attempt to blame us. Any oversights are your fault. Hopefully you will find a way to solve them in the pages ahead. There's also a couple of nice recipes to try, if you're feeling hungry after all that hard work.
We have also provided some very handy tips on Universe™ management strategies, global awarenesss, trouble hot spots, and good Galaxy™ initiatives.

Use the table below to find the problem you are looking for.

MISFORTUNE	FIXABLE?	SYMPTOM	SEE—
Old Age	YES	Time doesn't stop when persons sleep	Eternal Youth, page 59, *fig. 7*
Conflicts	YES	Very bad personality controls	Keep Everyone Happy, page 60
Crime	NO	Things inexplicably going missing	Crime Prevention Section, page 59, *fig. 4*
Exhaustion	YES	The complete inability to react to any given situation	Energy Equation, page 61, *fig. 19*
Cockroaches	NO	Evil insects terrorizing people	Controlling Your Life Forms, page 61
Failure	MAYBE	Being a complete and utter loser	Be Happy!, page 62, *fig. 11*
The Eighties	▓▓▓▓▓	A lot of people wearing clothes they shouldn't wear	▓▓▓▓▓
Bad Taste	NO	Very poor judgment in a number of situations	Good Taste Guide, page 61, *fig. 21*
Still Planets	PERHAPS	Planet spinning speed slows down	Spin Spin Spin Your Planets, page 62
Sprouts	YES *NO*	Strange vegetables growing in fields	Sprout Prevention, page 61, *fig. 5*

LUCIFER WAS HERE

HOW DO I COMPLETE THIS WITHOUT THE 8TH DAY? Golly

WITHOUT THE ANSWER, MY UNIVERSE IS DOOMED.

3 DAYS IN: MY PEOPLE ARE FIGHTING ALREADY → HOW DO I STOP THEM?

WHAT?

THE ANSWER IS FANTASTIC!!!

HAS ANYONE SEEN THESE PAGES? I REALLY REALLY NEED THEM, IT'S ALL GOING WRONG — WHERE ARE THESE PAGES I WILL PAY GOOD MONEY FOR THEM. – ROB. 0697 0392053961284

What does all this mean?

GIVE US TOMORROW OUR
GIVE US THIS TUESDAY OUR
GIVE US YESTERDAY OUR
GIVE US THIS DAY OUR   DAILY BREAD?

AND IT WAS GOOD...

Peace is such a Quality Idea.

Oh Ostriches

63

05 06 07 08 09 LEO 10 9 8 7 6 5 4 3 2 1

ISBN: 0-7407-5043-7

LIBRARY OF CONGRESS CONTROL NUMBER: 2004114039

CONGRATULATIONS!

As you have reached the end of this guide, you must be the proud new owner of your very own Universe™.

Please don't forget to register it as soon as possible, as unregistered Universes are likely to be destroyed by the Board of Space and Time™.

We, the Authors, want you to enjoy your newfound Creation. Please don't hestitate to contact us should you have any difficulties running your new Universe™. We understand there may be some initial glitches in the smooth operation of your Universe™, but would request that you consult the Eighth Day before calling us, as all the answers should be found there.

Once registered, your Universe™ will join all the other Universes already created and you will be invited to attend the bicentennial celebrations of Universe™ Creators at a random house somewhere in the Cosmos™.

We hope you have understood and enjoyed the activities of the past eight days and look forward to hearing from you in the not-too-distant future.

Good Luck,

The Authors

Glossary™

ANGRY THRONG OF PEOPLE
You know you have created this when your Persons™ begin sentences with phrases such as "For God's sake . . ." or "Bloody hell . . ." can be dealt with simply and effectively by consulting the Happy Person Maker™ in the Eighth Day.

CONCEPT OF RUST
A sign that time may not be on your side.

COW
Female. Generally not a particularly nice female.

INFORMATIVE PAMPHLETS
You can't beat some informative pamphlets. For details on production of especially informative pamhplets see the informative-pamphlet-production section of the Eighth Day.

LANDAU
Four-wheeled carriage with a folding hood.

LARGE LADLE
Rounded spatula (See spatula).

LARGER THAN LIFE
Big. Very big. I mean—like absolutely whopping.

MONDAYS
The wrong day to start work on. Making your people start the week on a Monday could prove disasterous.

OFF-SIDE RULE
Don't even attempt to explain when in the company of women.

ONE TOO MANY
Three too many—very good; two too many—good, but one too many—no. Just say no. No.

PROFESSIONAL LIQUID GLOSS
As professional a liquid gloss as you're likely to find—anywhere in the cosmos. Apply evenly for best results.

RELIGION
A great excuse to put your feet up on a Sunday. (See Sunday.)

SOLID CONVECTING MANTLE
A mantle for convecting matter such as solids.

SPATULA
Flattened ladle (See ladle).

SUNDAY
The eighth day of your week.

TEMPORARY CORNER LIGHTING
Casts a warming glow around a room. Try deploying a temporary corner light or three—you won't regret it.

TOTAL SATISFACTION
Oh, yes. That feeling when you see your planets assume that lovely oblong orbit around your sun.

THE INEVITABLE
A four-legged item that your persons will be able to sit around and enjoy inevidinner, inevilunch, inevibreakfast, or inevisupper.

THREE-PRONGED ATTACK
An attack branching from three equidistant prongs.

TRAJECTORY
The flight path of a tortoise.

TRUNDLE WHEEL
Get trundling.

UKULELE
An instrument which indeed appears to contain an abundance of vowels.

UNRIPE KUMQUATS
A fruit which in color and texture is not entirely dissimilar to that of a ripened kumquat in its early stages of development.

SELECTED BOOKS™ IN THE *HOW TO CREATE* SERIES AVAILBLE FROM GODFATHER PUBLICATIONS

THE PRICES SHOWN BELOW WERE CORRECT AT THE TIME OF GOING TO PRESS; HOWEVER, GODFATHER PUBLICATIONS RESERVES THE RIGHT TO SHOW NEW RETAIL PRICES ON COVERS THAT MAY DIFFER FROM THOSE PREVIOUSLY ADVERTISED IN THE TEXT OR ELSEWHERE.

3X5D8	2	HOW TO CREATE A BEAUTIFUL MOMENT	$14.95
4E9K2	3	HOW TO CREATE THE ULTIMATE BLACK HOLE	$16.95
S24H2	4	HOW TO CREATE SUPREME SUPERPEOPLE	$19.95
3F0P9	5	HOW TO CREATE THE PERFECT CHEESEBOARD	$9.95
4K3R1	1	HOW TO CREATE A SIMPLE LIFE	$21.95
2G2A1	9	HOW TO CREATE PROPER ANTI-MATTER	$4.95
8X5W1	4	HOW TO CREATE AN AIR OF MYSTERY	$19.95
4R6Y0	3	HOW TO CREATE A LOGICAL CONCLUSION	$1.50

QUALITY BOOK. BUY THIS BOOK BUY IT!

All Godfather Publication titles are available from:
Unreal Book Shops, PO Box One
Neither credit cards nor cash are accepted. Please telephone *800 I want to buy a book*.
Free postage and packing in this cosmos.

Customers from other cosmi, please allow $799.08 per book.

Available from all good bookshops now!

Trademarks™

Big Bang, Universe, Planet, Cosmic Glow, Waters, Sky, Vacuum, Weather, Landmass, Vegetation
Galaxy, Star Systems, Time, Sea Creature, Species, Person, Animal, Creation, Alphabet,
Equation of Purity, Halo, Euphoria, Infinity, Harmony, Trademark, The Answer

WHERE/WHAT

Register Your Universe ™

|2|

The Board of Space and Time
FREEPOST
PO Box 1

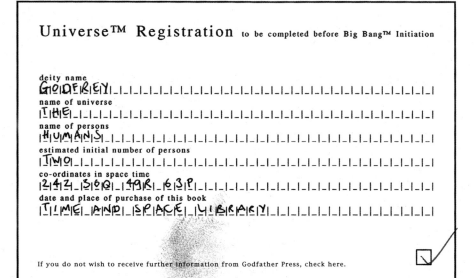

Universe™ Registration to be completed before Big Bang™ Initiation

deity name
|G|O|D|F|R|E|Y|_|_|_|_|_|_|_|_|_|_|_|_|_|_|_|_|_|_|_|_|_|_|_|_|_|_|_|_|_|_|_|_|_|_|_|_|_|_|

name of universe
|T|H|E|_|_|_|_|_|_|_|_|_|_|_|_|_|_|_|_|_|_|_|_|_|_|_|_|_|_|_|_|_|_|_|_|_|_|_|_|_|_|_|_|_|_|_|

name of persons
|H|U|M|A|N|S|_|_|_|_|_|_|_|_|_|_|_|_|_|_|_|_|_|_|_|_|_|_|_|_|_|_|_|_|_|_|_|_|_|_|_|_|_|_|_|

estimated initial number of persons
|T|W|O|_|_|_|_|_|_|_|_|_|_|_|_|_|_|_|_|_|_|_|_|_|_|_|_|_|_|_|_|_|_|_|_|_|_|_|_|_|_|_|_|_|_|

co-ordinates in space time
|2|4|7|_|5|0|Q|_|4|9|R|_|6|3|P|_|_|_|_|_|_|_|_|_|_|_|_|_|_|_|_|_|_|_|_|_|_|_|_|_|_|_|_|_|

date and place of purchase of this book
|T|I|M|E|_|A|N|D|_|S|P|A|C|E|_|L|I|B|R|A|R|Y|_|_|_|_|_|_|_|_|_|_|_|_|_|_|_|_|_|_|_|_|_|

If you do not wish to receive further information from Godfather Press, check here. ☑